Learn How to Play th

ASAP

Irish Mandolin

by Doc Rossi

ISBN 978-1-57424-303-1
SAN 683-8022

Cover by James Creative Group

CONTENTS

INCRODUCCION

Irish music was once an essentially rural tradition, becoming urbanized as country people moved to town. With urbanization came a blending of styles and an ever-growing market. Michael Colman was one of Irish traditional music's first international stars, and The Chieftains, Planxty, De Dannan and The Bothy Band led a wave of early pioneers who made Irish traditional music a vibrant part of the world music scene. These groups and their popularity inspired the countless groups that have followed in their wakes all over the world, bringing not only changes to the music, but new instruments, adding guitar, bouzouki, cittern and mandolin to the ranks of fiddles, banjos, whistles, flutes, and pipes. Notable mandolin players in Irish traditional music are Andy Irvine, Johnny Moynihan, Paul Brady, Mick Moloney, Kevin MacLeod and Séamus Egan.

The defining characteristics of Irish traditional music are its richly developed sense of melody coupled with quick, danceable rhythms. Although there are exceptions, Irish tunes tend to be modal, and often follow their own logic rather than that of conventional major and minor scales. Dance tunes are embellished with a variety of ornaments, occasional harmonies and variation. The basic types of tune are reels, jigs, hornpipes and polkas.

The tunes in this book have been arranged by genre and in order of difficulty. Because ornamentation plays such an important role in Irish music, before getting to the tunes we'll have a look at some of the most common ornaments and how to play them on the mandolin.

Ornamentation in traditional music is improvised and spontaneous. Most ornaments on the mandolin are played using hammer-ons and pull-offs, with the occasional slide. Ornaments should be played quickly, without putting the other notes in the bar out of time. In other words, they "borrow" time from the notes near them. They are really just a flick of a left-hand finger and should add bounce and lightness to the tune. The exception to this is the plucked triplet, which is primarily a right-hand ornament. It too should also be played with lightness and bounce, and often has a more percussive or rhythmic rather than melodic effect.

Drones on the mandolin are played by sounding an open string and letting it ring while the melody continues. **CD track 1** illustrates the use of drones in the A music of "Saddle the Pony."

Double stopping is playing two notes simultaneously on adjacent strings. The added note is often a harmony note, but one of the most common double stops is playing the same note on two strings. On the mandolin this is done by sliding a finger up to the seventh fret to produce a double D or A or E. **CD track 2** gives an example of double stopping in "Farewell to Whisky."

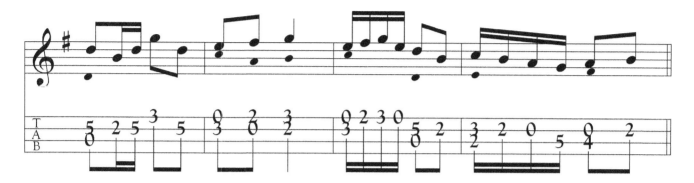

A **single grace** note is written as a small eighth note, sometimes with a line through its stem. They are often placed between notes of the same pitch, or before an important note to give it more emphasis. Pick the grace and pull-off for the main note. The first example, from "Cooley's Reel," uses a note one fret above the main note. [**CD track 3**]

This phrase from "Saddle the Pony" uses single grace notes two frets above the main note. [CD track 4]

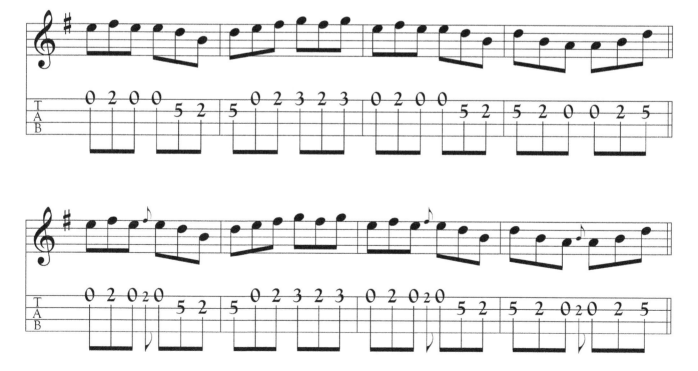

A single grace note three frets above the main note is used in "Farewell to Whisky"
[CD track 5]

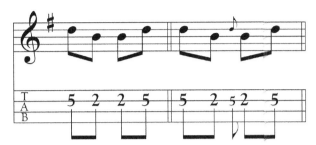

Double grace notes or trills are written as two sixteenth notes. Pick the first note, then quickly hammer-on and pull-off the next two. The first example is from "Cooley's Reel." [CD Track 6]

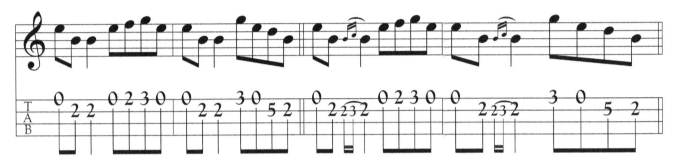

Here is an example from "The Banshee" using a note three frets above the main note.
[CD track 7]

Finally, here is the second part of "The Banshee" played using single and double grace notes. [CD track 8]

Triplets are three notes played in the place of two. They are often used to decorate longer notes or to fill-in between notes that are more than a step apart. The first examples are from jigs. The dotted quarter note in measure 3 of "Gallagher's Frolics" could be broken up into an eighth note plus an eight-note triplet in place of the remaining two eighth notes. [CD track 9]

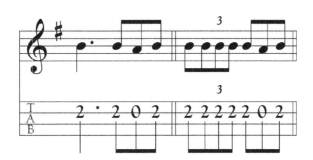

Another common use of triplets in jigs is found in this example from "Tripping Up the Stairs" [CD track 10]

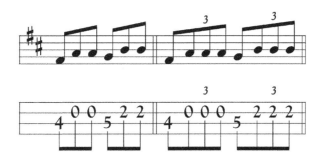

Returning to the phrase from "Saddle the Pony" used to illustrate single grace notes [CD track 4], we can hear the same phrase played using triplets. [CD track 11]

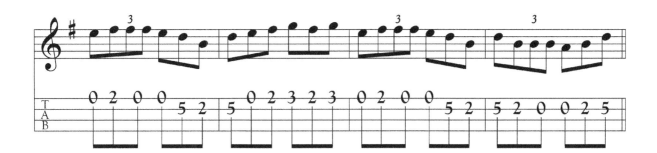

Triplets are often used in hornpipes to fill in between adjacent notes in a melody that are three or more frets apart. Here are several ways of interpreting a line from "The Star of Munster." [CD track 12]

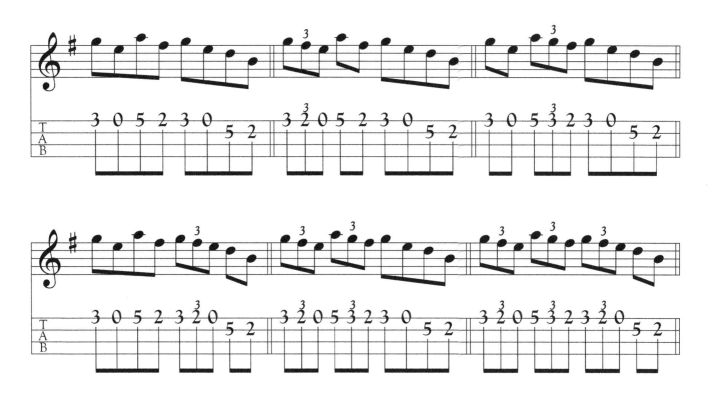

To finish our look at triplets, here is a well-known example from "The Rights of Man." [CD track 13]

Rolls or **turns** are four- or five-note ornaments that use the notes just above and below the main note. They can be used to decorate quarter notes and dotted quarter notes, or a group of quarter and eighth notes of the same pitch. **CD track 14** shows how the previous example from "Gallagher's Frolics" [CD track 9] might be played using a roll rather than a triplet.

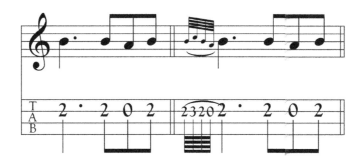

CD track 15 shows how a phrase from "The Banshee" used in CD track 8 might be rolled.

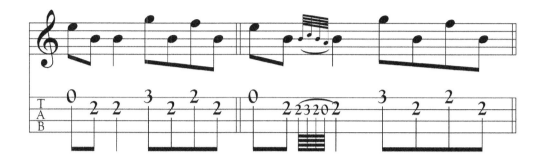

Finally, a word about the different types of tune presented in this book. We start with polkas because they often provide the simplest melodies. They have two beats to the bar and often have a dotted feel or swing to them where the first note is slightly longer than the others.

Hornpipes seem to have started off in England. They are usually written in common time but can have an almost funky 2/4 feel. They are sometimes written with dotted notes, but I find it more clear to write them as straight eights and play with swing.

Jigs are in 6/8 time. They can be counted 123 456, but the feel is really two groups of three. You can think of jig rhythm as a shuffle - long short / long short. There are different ways to pick jigs; the two most common are down-up-down/down-up-down and down-up-down/up-down-up, with string crossings sometimes breaking the pattern. I favor the first pattern because I like the drive it naturally has, but it does have the awkward feature of consecutive downstrokes, which can sometimes be tricky in quick tunes. In addition to adding more drive and interest, ornaments can also make a tricky passage easier to play by breaking the picking pattern with hammer-ons, pull-offs or plucked triplets.

"The Humours of Whisky" is a slip jig. Slip jigs and hop jigs are in 9/8 time - three beats per measure with the dotted quarter having one beat.

Reels are straight 4/4, often played quite quickly, and for this reason are not usually played with as much swing as the other types of tune.

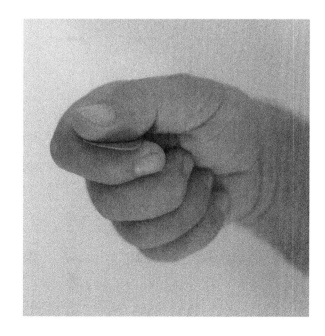

Dan Coakley's Polka

[CD track 16]

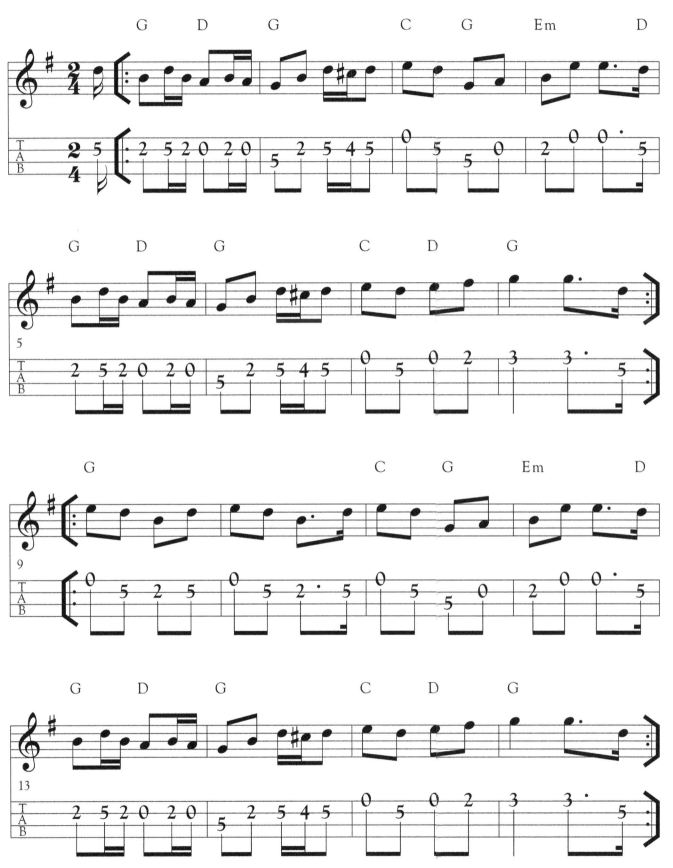

FAREWELL TO WHISKY

[CD track 17]

Dennis Murphy's Polka

[CD track 18]

12

SEAN RYAN'S POLKA

[CD track 19]

ᴄɪss ᴄᴜʀᴘʜʏ

O'Carolan

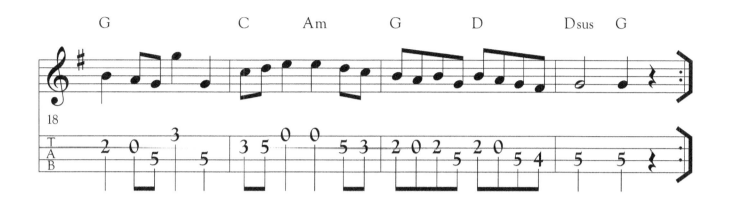

KING OF THE FAIRIES

[CD track 21]

16

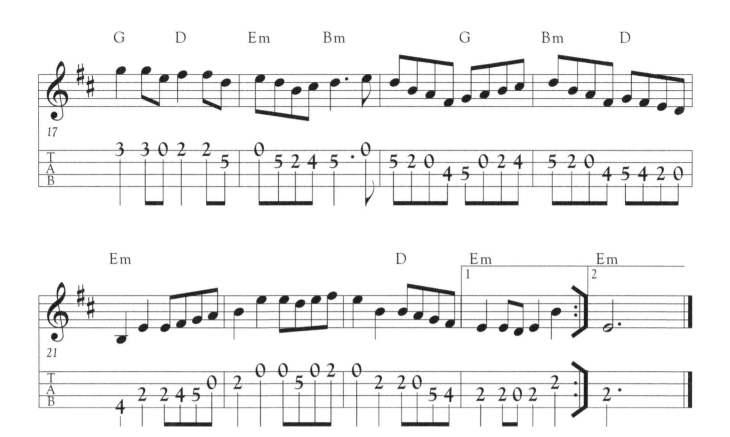

chief o'neill's favourite
the flowers of adrigole

[CD track 22]

THE RIGHTS OF MAN

[CD track 23]

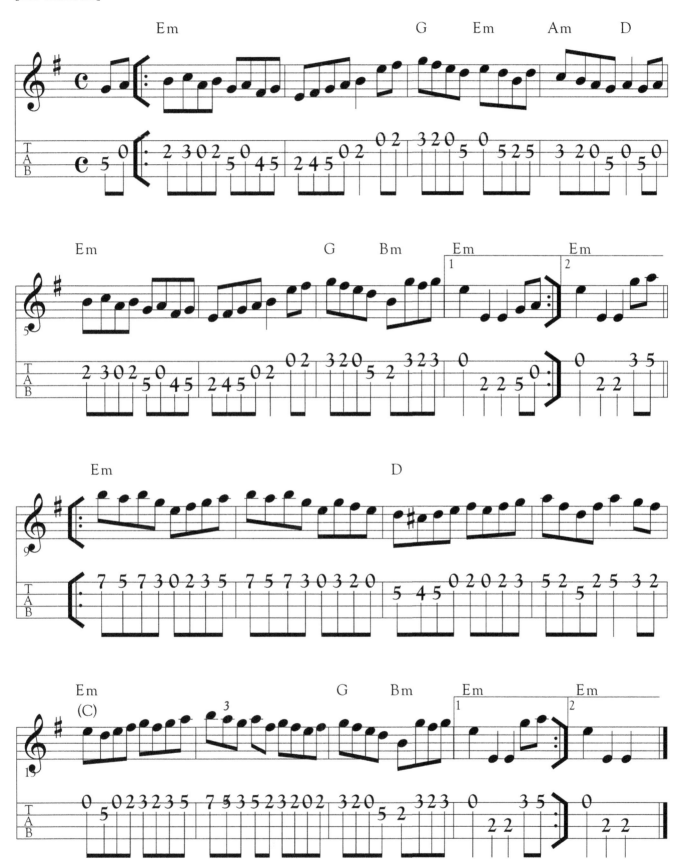

saddle the pony

[CD track 24]

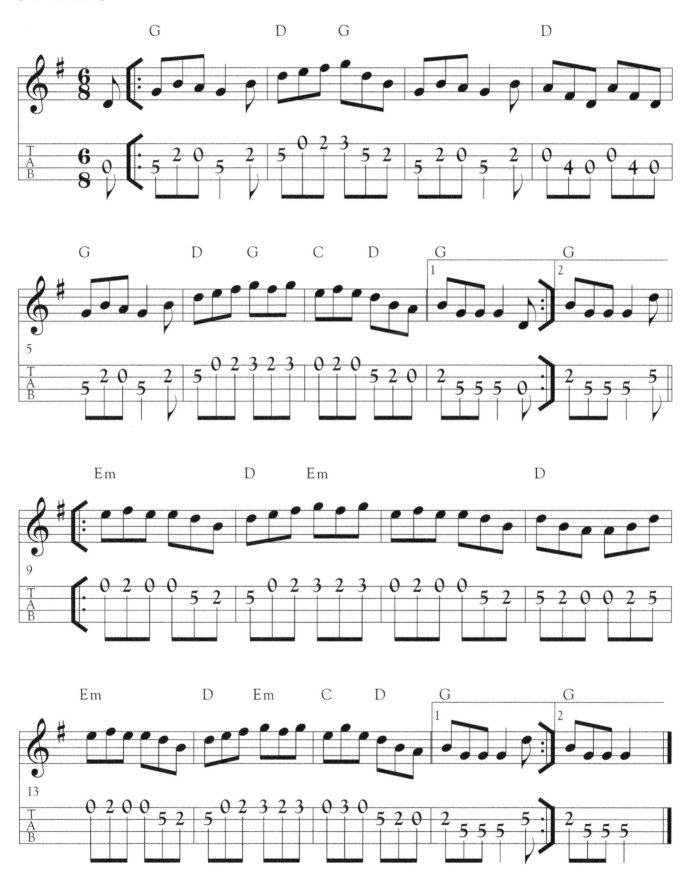

TRIPPING UP THE STAIRS

[CD track 25]

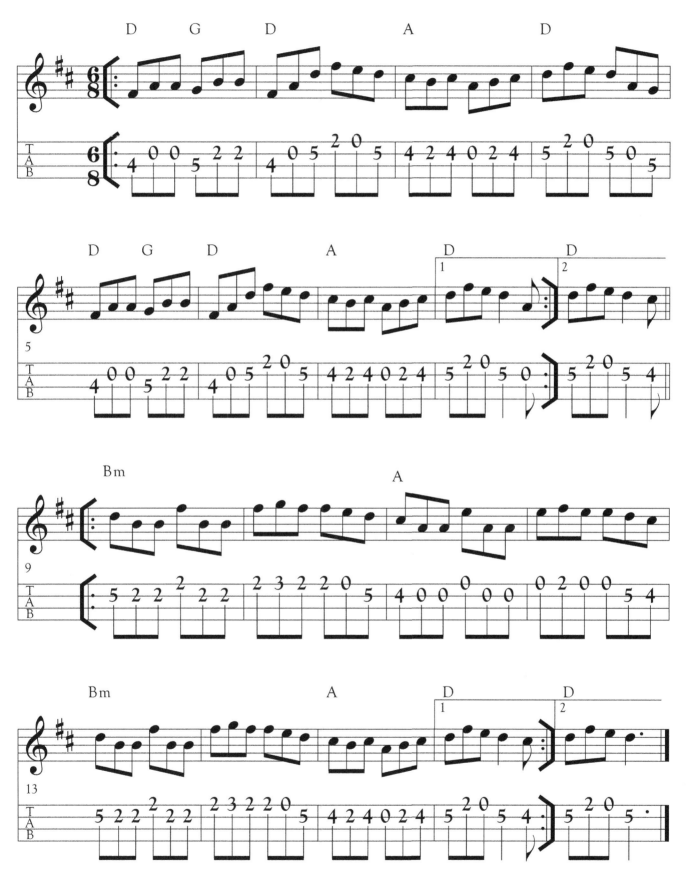

haste to the wedding

[CD track 26]

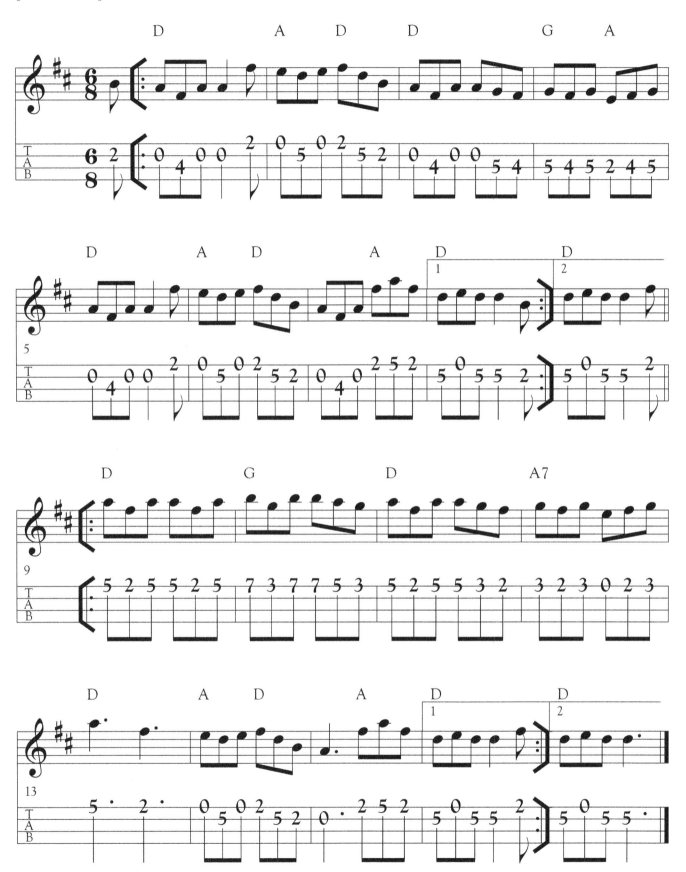

GALLACHER'S FROLICS

23

the irish washerwoman

[CD track 28]

24

the kesh jig
kerrigan's jig

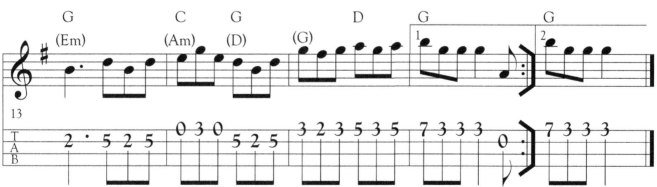

the humours of whisky

[CD track 30]

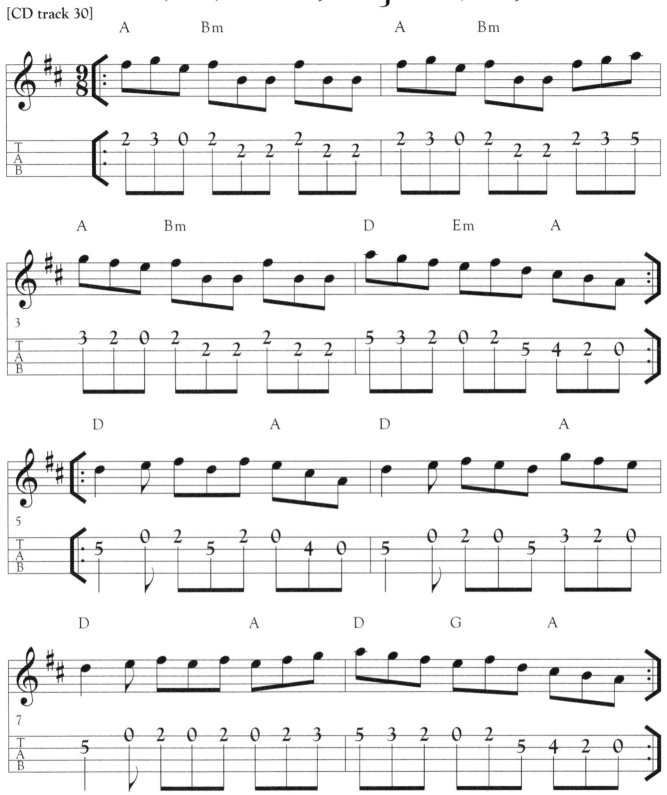

Drowsy Maggie

the BANSHEE

[CD track 32]

cooley's reel

[CD track 33]

the scar of munscer

[CD track 34]

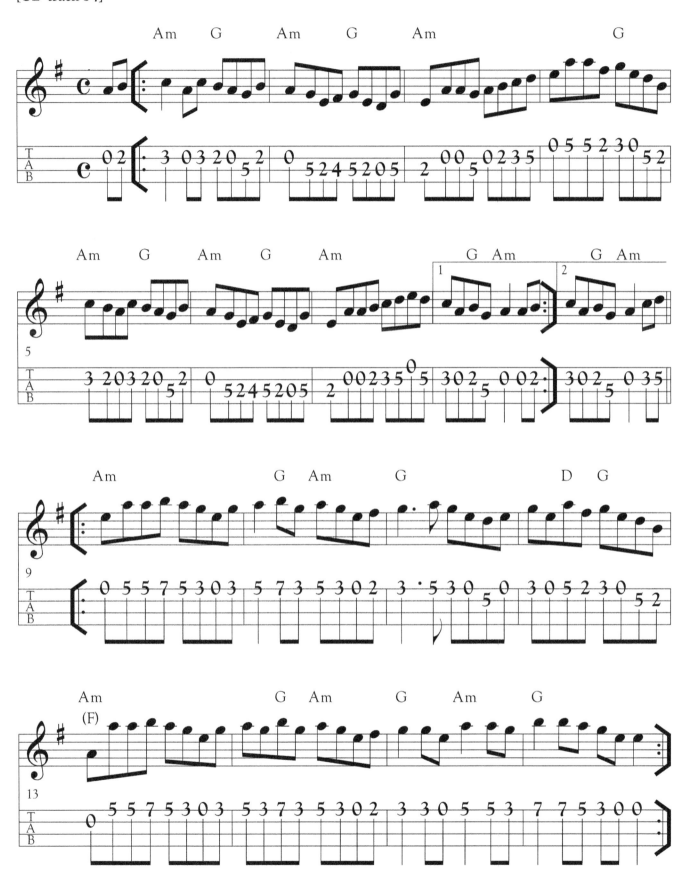

the maid behind the bar

[CD track 35]

CD TRACK LIST

1. Using Drone Strings
2. Double Stops
3. Single Grace Note ex. 1
4. Single Grace Note ex. 2
5. Single Grace Note ex. 3
6. Double Grace Note ex. 1
7. Double Grace Note ex. 2
8. Single and Double Graces combined
9. Triplets ex. 1
10. Triplets ex. 2
11. Triplets ex. 3
12. Triplets ex. 4
13. Triplets ex. 5
14. Rolls ex. 1
15. Rolls ex. 2
16. Dan Croakley's Polka
17. Farewell to Whisky
18. Dennis Murphy's Polka
19. Sean Ryan's Polka
20. Miss Murphy
21. The King of the Fairies
22. Chief O'Neill's Favourite
23. The Rights of Man
24. Saddle the Pony
25. Tripping Up the Stairs
26. Haste to the Wedding
27. Gallagher's Frolics
28. The Irish Washerwoman
29. The Kesh Jig
30. The Humours of Whisky
31. Drowsy Maggie
32. The Banshee
33. Cooley's Reel
34. The Star of Munster
35. The Maid Behind the Bar

More Great Books from Doc Rossi...

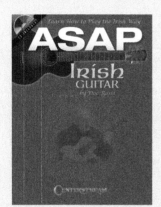

ASAP IRISH GUITAR
Learn How to Play the Irish Way
by Doc Rossi

This quick guide to flatpicking Irish traditional music was written by Doc Rossi, a well-known citternist and guitarist in both traditional and early music. He's created this book for intermediate to advanced players who want to improve their technique, develop ideas and learn new repertoire. Starting with the basics of technique and ornamentation in traditional music, Doc then goes directly into the tunes, in standard notation and tab. Focusing on traditional music from Ireland, Doc has also chosen tunes from England, France, Flanders, North America and Corsica to reflect the guitar's broad range. Right- and left-hand techniques, ornamentation, arranging and other topics are taught through the tunes themselves. Doc has developed his own tuning for playing traditional music, and this book shows you how to use it. His tuning makes it easy to play tunes in all the important traditional keys without moving a capo around or having to negotiate difficult position shifts, while at the same time providing a number of open strings and other possibilities for playing your own accompaniment. An audio CD with all of the tunes played at medium tempo is included..

00113683 Book/CD Pack $19.99

CELTIC CITTERN
by Doc Rossi

Although the cittern has a history spanning 500 years and several countries, like its cousin the Irish bouzouki, it is a relative newcomer to contemporary traditional music. Doc Rossi, a well-known citternist in both traditional and early music, has created this book for intermediate to advanced players who want to improve their technique, develop ideas and learn new repertoire. Guitarists can play all of the tunes in this book on the guitar by tuning C F C G C F, low to high, and putting a capo at the second fret. The lowest line in the tablature then corresponds to the fifth string. The CD features all the tunes played at a medium tempo.

00001460 Book/CD Pack $19.99

CELTIC GUITAR
by Doc Rossi

Doc Rossi, a well-known citternist and guitarist in traditional and early music, has created this book for intermediate to advanced players wishing to improve their technique and learn new repertoire. He's chosen tunes from England, France, Flanders, North America and Corsica to reflect the broad range of the instrument. He teaches right- and left-hand techniques, ornamentation, arranging and other topics, as well as his own unique tuning to make playing traditional music easier. The CD features all of the tunes played at medium tempo.

00001513 Book/CD Pack $19.99

P.O. Box 17878 - Anaheim Hills, CA 92817
(714) 779-9390   www.centerstream-usa.com

More Great Mandolin Books from Centerstream...

More Great Guitar Books from Centerstream...

ASAP POWER PICKING
For Electric and Acoustic Guitars

by David Brewster This book will help beginning guitarists "find" the strings of the guitar through a series of basic (yet melodic) picking exercises. As you become more comfortable striking the strings of the guitar with a pick using the exercises and examples here, you should eventually create your own variations and picking exercises.

00001330 Book/CD Pack...$15.99

LATIN STYLES FOR GUITAR

by Brian Chambouleyron

A dozen intermediate to advanced originals in notes & tab display various Latin American styles. For each, the CD features the lead part as well as an accompaniment-only rhythm track for play along.

00001123 Book/CD Pack $19.95

BEBOP GUITAR
Basic Theory and Practice for Jazz Guitar in the Style of Charlie Parker

by Joseph Weidlich

This book/CD pack shows guitarists how to transform basic jazz improv techniques into bebop figures in Bird's famous "with strings" style by making chromatic and rhythmic alterations. Includes many musical examples, most in the user-friendly key of G major, to accommodate players not well versed in jazz flat keys.

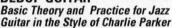

00001196 Book/CD Pack $25.95

GUITAR TUNING FOR THE COMPLETE MUSICAL IDIOT

by Ron Middlebrook

There's nothing more distracting than hearing a musician play out of tune. This user-friendly book/DVD pack teaches various methods for tuning guitars – even 12-strings! – and basses, including a section on using electronic tuning devices. Also covers intonation, picks, changing strings, and much more!

00000002 Book/DVD Pack...$16.95
00001198 DVD $10.00

ASAP CLASSICAL GUITAR
Learn How to Play the Classical Way

by James Douglas Esmond

Teacher-friendly or for self-study, this book/CD pack for beginning to intermediate guitarists features classical pieces and exercises presented progressively in notes and tab, with each explained thoroughly and performed on the accompanying CD. A great way to learn to play ASAP!

00001202 Book/CD Pack $15.95

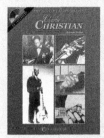

THE GUITAR CHORD SHAPES OF CHARLIE CHRISTIAN

by Joe Weidlich

Chord shapes are moveable; thus one can play the riffs in virtually any key without difficulty by simply moving the shape, and fingerings used to play them, up or down the fingerboard. The author shows how the chord shapes – F, D and A – are formed, then can easily be modified to major, minor, dominant seventh and diminished seventh chord voicings. The identifiable "sound" of a particular lick is preserved regardless of how many notes are added on either side of it, e.g., pickup notes or tag endings. Many examples are shown and played on the CD of how this basic concept was used by Charlie Christian.

00000388 Book/CD Pack $19.95

THE COUNTRY GUITAR STYLE OF CHARLIE MONROE
Based on the 1936-1938 Bluebird Recordings by The Monroe Brothers

by Joseph Weidlich

This great overview of Charlie Monroe's unique guitar performance style (he used just his thumb and index finger) presents 52 songs, with an in-depth look at the backup patterns & techniques from each chord family (G, F, D, C, E, A), plus special note sequences, common substitutions and stock backup phrases. Includes the bluegrass classics "Roll in My Sweet Baby's Arms," "My Long Journey Home" and "Roll On, Buddy," plus a discography and complete Bluebird recording session info.

00001305 ....$19.99

ASAP GUITARIST GUIDE TO STRING BENDING & VIBRATO
Learn How to Bend the Correct Way

by Dave Brewster

String bending and vibrato are two of the most popular guitar techniques used in all musical styles, yet for most beginning and intermediate players, gaining control of them might seem overwhelming. This book outlines some of the most common bending and vibrato techniques and licks, teaching them in an easy-to-digest manner to help you see and hear how to use them with confidence in a musical context. Contains more than 150 helpful examples!

00001347 Book/CD Pack $19.99

HYMNS AND SPIRITUALS FOR FINGERSTYLE GUITAR

by James Douglas Esmond

Originating in the South during the antebellum days on the old plantations, at religious revivals and at camp meetings, hymns and spirituals are the native folk songs of our own America. This collection features 13 songs, some with two arrangements – one easy, the second more difficult. Songs include: Were You There? • Steal Away • Amazing Grace • Every Time I Feel the Spirit • Wade in the Water • and more.

00001183 Book/CD Pack $19.95

P.O. Box 17878 - Anaheim Hills, CA 92817
(714) 779-9390   www.centerstream-usa.com